A Pioneer Alaskan's Lifetime of Rhymes and Lines

Frank Wilton Sharp

ISBN: 978-0-578-40859-0
Library of Congress Control Number: 2018962824

Financial support for this book was generously provided by Larry Calvin of Sitka, Alaska.
Original cover painting by Joann George.
Book design by Peter Bradley.
Manuscript preparation and maps by Mim McConnell, Shelter Cove Publishing.
QR codes, scanned by a smartphone application, provide oration by Frank Sharp.

Printed by Lulu Press Inc. in the United States of America.

First printing edition 2018.

Island Institute dba Island Institute Press
PO Box 2420
Sitka, Alaska 99835

www.iialaska.org
director@islandinstitutealaska.org

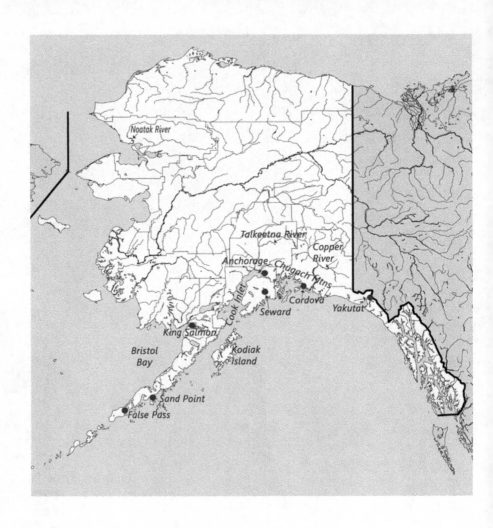

State of Alaska

These maps show locations mentioned in Frank Sharp's writings.

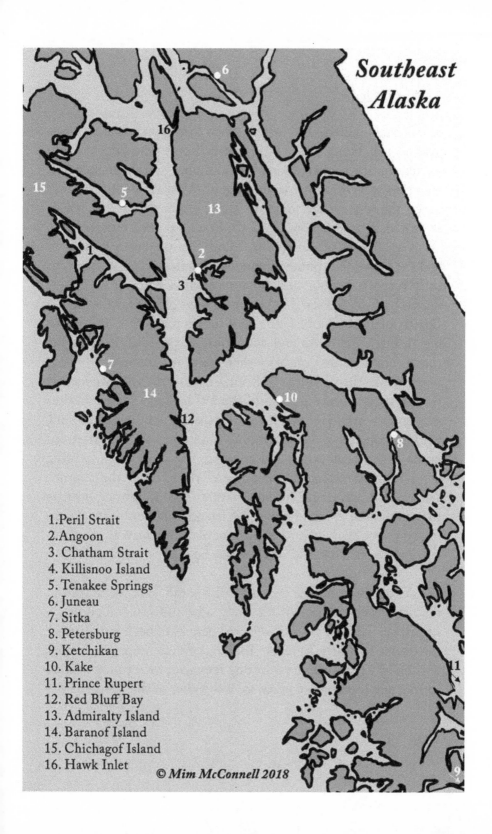

Southeast
Alaska

1. Peril Strait
2. Angoon
3. Chatham Strait
4. Killisnoo Island
5. Tenakee Springs
6. Juneau
7. Sitka
8. Petersburg
9. Ketchikan
10. Kake
11. Prince Rupert
12. Red Bluff Bay
13. Admiralty Island
14. Baranof Island
15. Chichagof Island
16. Hawk Inlet

© Mim McConnell 2018

Editor's Note

It was back in 2016 that Larry Calvin first approached me, suggesting that Frank Sharp is an Alaskan poet who people ought to take notice of, that Frank had captured stories in rhyme of an important time in the forging of Alaska's identity. Larry paved the way for me to get to know Frank over the course of several visits to Angoon. Through Frank's poetry, I've gotten to know a different side of Alaska. Frank Sharp grew up moving to and fro across the country, living in 30 states. He had spent his early years in Angoon and Tenakee Springs and was ultimately drawn back to Alaska. He became a boat officer for the Alaska Department of Fish & Game and then a protection officer, rising through the ranks and with more responsibilities over the years. Frank retired on his father's land in Angoon. For four years he was the president of Kootznoowoo, the village corporation established as a product of the 1971 Alaska Native Claims Settlement Act. He's spent the years since tending to his land, working long days on the winding road down to his waterfront home and nearby cabin, and enjoying the fruits of it: hunting octopus at the minus tide, picking endless berries in the summer, salmon and halibut fishing in Chatham Strait, hunting deer on the mountaintops, and helping his friends and family see Alaska the way that he does... as a spiritual place, a reservoir of silence that he thinks the world will one day be ready to turn to.

Frank calls himself "the mouth of the south." He has stories to tell from every minute of his lively, adventurous, and endlessly surprising life. The poems collected here have been written over the course of nearly 70 years. The first of these were love poems, written by Frank as a globetrotting teenager; for a young woman he met at a high school party, for a member of the Women's Air

Force who he had spotted on the base in Germany, for the third cousin who he met in Scotland while on furlough.

As he settled down in Alaska with his wife Alice, the poems shifted to match his adventurous spirit. As an enforcement officer in the early days of statehood, Frank roved the wilds of Alaska while forging deep friendships with community members and colleagues wherever he went. He wrote extensively about wilderness, about adventure, about friendship, and about work and duty. Each of those broad themes is represented by a section in this collection.

The introduction is a transcription of hours of Frank telling the story of his life in all its dimensions. The words are Frank's. The poems and stories are transcribed as he provided them, written in varied forms over the years on whatever was handy. QR codes, scanned by a smartphone application, will take the reader to Frank Sharp reciting his work.

Says Frank, "My friend Dennis, he always tells me, 'Frank, you're a me, me, me person.'" "You know what Dennis? You're right. But who's more important than me?"

- Peter Bradley

Introduction

I was born on the 14th of February, 1932. Valentine's Day. In Orofino, Idaho, which in Spanish means fine gold. Oro-Fino.

My mother was Mary-Ellen Coghill. She married Albert Thomas Sharp, a half-breed Tlingit Indian from Alaska. On his other side he was Canadian, of Berwick, New Brunswick. The Sharps.

Wilton is a family name that has been passed down in the Sharp family. In Berwick, many of the stores, drugstores, barbershops, everything, are Sharp. The Sharps originated in England and half of them dropped off in New Jersey and the others stayed loyal to the king, Loyalists, and because they stayed loyal to King Frederick (sic) of England, they were given a thousand acres of land in the Berwick area, which they farmed and which they still have possession of today.

My grandfather on my mother's side, Sinclair Coghill, who all of my life I called Dede, emigrated when he was 15 years old from Hamilton, Scotland. My grandmother was from Wisconsin, and we have a famous background because her mother was a Drake, and we're relatives of Sir Francis Drake. Somewhere around the house here we have silver spoons with the Drake family name carved on them.

My grandfather James Wilton Sharp, and his brother Frank, came to Alaska when they were 20-some years old to mine gold; they helped build the Chilkoot Trail. Frank did really well mining, he built hotels in Anchorage and Fairbanks, and for some reason, I don't know what happened to my grandpa, but he ended up down here in Angoon, Alaska. He started a ranch, and had oxen (Buck and Bright), cattle, pigs and chickens, and supplied the community of Killisnoo Island, which had a population then of around 1500 I'm told; it was a whaling station, black cod, and herring plants, over the years. And he married my grandmother, Mary Nelson, a full-blooded Tlingit Indian, and he was 34 and she was 14.

The town of Killisnoo burned down in 1922. He sold the farm to a guy named Knutson, 58 acres in Hood Bay, and he never got paid. My dad and all of his brothers and sisters were born there. My grandfather's wife had left him, so he took the children down south to Seattle, put the children temporarily in an orphanage while he went looking for work. One of the boys, Frank, was playing on a railroad track and got run over by the train.

My grandfather went over into Idaho, around Orofino, on the Clearwater River, and became a logger. When he could afford it, he brought his family over. My dad (Albert Thomas Sharp) was 18, my mother was 17, when they got married. First they produced a daughter, who died at age 6 months, Alberta, and then I came along in 1932. My memories probably start about 10 or 11 years old. That goes back to many bad memories. Poverty. Complete poverty. Alcoholism. Things that no child should ever experience. My dad and mother divorced when I was 12 years old. And then my mother remarried - a man from Tenakee, and that was the same kind of situation. But years later she married an-

"Frankie" in Angoon 1938

9

other man, and then we started travelling. I claim I've lived in over 30 states. He was a lithographer, a color printer, an expert at it; he could get a job anywhere. We travelled extensively all over the United States.

****

During World War II, as a waitress in a restaurant, my mother had it all arranged. I could go down to the restaurant that she either ran or where she was a waitress. The waitresses all knew me, they'd say, "Oh Frank, you're here for your roast pork and apple sauce?" My favorite!

Often soldiers would wake me up in the morning... and we didn't have any money. You know, sometimes we didn't have anything to eat. I saw things that no kid, no child should ever see. And when I was being molested, they were so busy out there doing their thing, drinking and chasing around. They don't even know it today, that's the thing you don't talk about much. The result is that you're growing something, you know? And it made me what I am today. You have to be strong, and just keep moving on, kind of thing. I love my mother, but she wasn't really a woman who should have had any children.

She sent me down about six times during the war, to my grandparents in Orofino, Idaho, and they owned a store and a really nice house... and were members in different organizations. They were upstanding people in town, owning a clothing store and everything. That's the only time I had what I would call a home life.

We moved around so much. I say 30 states. I know we were in Minnesota, Nebraska, California, Oregon, Kansas, Missouri,

Texas; it goes on and on.

****

I was in Tenakee Springs from 1935 to 1945. A couple of years ago, the historical society came over and interviewed me, and I told them of the people that were there when I was there during the war. What happened is that Tenakee had two big canneries, so all of Angoon people basically lived in Tenakee at those canneries and worked in the canneries. When they closed down, they came back to Angoon. Same thing with Hood Bay, and Chatham cannery, right across Chatham Strait from here. We also worked at Hawk Inlet. Everybody worked in the canneries in the summertime.

If you knew my background and you looked at me today, it's a miracle.

****

I was an extremely lonely child, no friends. So I had a lot of time to be sad, I guess. Because you could never make any friends, moving, moving, moving, moving. Finally we ended up in Kansas City, Missouri. It was the same there, but I joined up with a good friend, John "Blackie" Henderson, and we became gangsters. I was his bodyguard.

John Henderson was my friend. But he was also... he was a really good artist, by the way. He drew crime magazine things. A really good artist. But he was the boss, and we would pull small jobs, and then we would buy hamburgers up the gazoo, a lot of hamburgers. But he was always mad at somebody, you know? So we'd go to a hamburger joint someplace where this guy was and when he went to the toilet we'd go in and lock the door and knock out his teeth and beat him to a pulp. I would do anything John asked me to. I packed twin .38 revolvers. And one time, in a theater (we were going to movies a lot) the cops knew about us, and so they came in. I had to hand off my pistols to somebody else, and they searched me. Another time, we had a gun, it was a .22, and supposedly single fire. But somehow he had somebody make it up into an automatic; it would fire 7 shots at once; you had to move this little pin. The stock was made to look like a machine gun. So I'm walking down the street with it, and the cops stop me, and they're looking at it "is it an auto?", "no, not an automatic", you know, and they didn't discover that there's a little pin you push and then it would go "pff!" seven shots at a time.

I dyed my hair red, peroxided it. When you take black hair, the first thing it does is turn red, and you leave it too long and it would turn white. I was known as "Red". I was a redhead for a long time, by peroxiding. Everybody thought I was a redhead!

Finally, my folks were leaving, and I decided to join the Air Force. I went into the Air Force and was in there four years, made Sergeant, was in Germany for almost four years. Wonderful. I travelled all over Europe, and then came back to the United States.
****

Arriving in Germany, we landed in

Frank Sharp, Air Force

Bremerhaven, and then they took us by train up to Marburg.

In Marburg, I would say many women would meet the ships. Girls everywhere, they were hungry. You could buy a whole family for a lump of coal, you could. And we'd killed all of their men. Mostly women and their girls lived.

I went into the Air Force and had nice clothes and a nice room and good food… and within a year, a year and a half, I made Sergeant. Next thing I know, I'm Staff Sergeant in charge of a communications center, travelling all over the world on free Air Force hops, that sort of thing. It just absolutely changed me.

To many I was a high school dropout. I didn't study for the GED, I was a flunk in all of my grades, I had seven study halls because we'd get in trouble drinking in classes. I think the highest grade I got was a C+, and that was probably in gym. But you know what I was? I was a track star! I took second place in the state championships in the mile, in 1948, in Missouri! I went to Central High School in Kansas City, and I was a runner. I ran the mile and the 440, and that one night I ran the 440 in about 44, and then I ran the mile and I lost by 5/10ths of a second. I was second in the mile. I used to run all the time, even in Anchorage in my 50's, I liked to run. I beat all of the guys in the academy, and I was 40 years old! I could run a 5-minute mile easy.

I was always thinking of coming back to Alaska. Over there, the head general of all of Europe interviewed me… they were concerned, because most of the guys that had been in for 4 or 5 years were leaving. They were setting up meetings, because they were losing their trained people, they weren't re-enlisting.

And he called me in, the head general of all of Europe, and he's talking with me, him and me and the stenographer. And I was telling him about how I would come back to Alaska, get a GI loan, buy a fishing boat, and he tells the stenographer, "Stop taking notes". And I tell him all about what I want to do when I go back to Alaska, and he says, "I don't blame you." His job was to talk me into staying in the Air Force, and when I tell him what I want to do in Alaska, he tells me he doesn't blame me!

I left the Air Force in August 1953. I'd spent 18 months in Berlin and 17 months in Wiesbaden. I'd been a teletype operator, which I trained for in Cheyenne, Wyoming. Don't ever go to Cheyenne, Wyoming. It's so windy there, it's unbelievable. Miserable. We lived in barracks and we burned coal, there was coal dust everywhere. The locals wouldn't let us anywhere near the girls. We spent 18 weeks learning how to type, send faxes, Morse code. I'd never ever typed.

***

Then it's time to go home. We took a ship. Came across.

I was engaged to a Scotch girl, my third cousin, Jean. My folks had moved from Kansas City to San Diego. They only pay you where you sign up, your home of record. I'd signed up in Kansas City, but my folks had moved, so I went to San Diego, because that's where they were, in Harbison Canyon. Next door was Alice and Jerry Klipp, and their two sons, Tommy and Terry, 13 and 11. We had a little bar in the canyon where we all hung out.

Alice was next door. Jerry, he delivered 7-Up and Pepsi; he had a truck. She told me later her husband had a trapline of women; he'd go to all of these places. We would hang out in this one bar and drink beer and dance, and I finally told my mother, "I've got to leave, because I'm in love with Alice." I left, and we wrote each other. I have all the letters upstairs, and I wrote telling her that I made over a thousand dollars a year… and so we write. I was an avid boxer in the Air Force, and she'd watch those Saturday night fights on the TV. You'd have these fights - one fighter wore black and one wore white. So we'd start exchanging quarters as to who won - I couldn't see it, she could see it on her TV. And I'd say, "Well I take black", or whatever, and she'd send me a letter, "You won", or "You lost, you owe me a quarter", so we were writing! We were writing.

I was fishing on my uncle's seine boat in the summer and I get a telegram at Hawk Inlet cannery, and it's from my mother, says "We'll be in at 3:30 this afternoon with Alice and her boys." Holy smokes! I was nothing. And when you're in the cannery, there's just so many little shacks for the workers, and they're taken! Luckily my uncle knew the superintendent, Mut Stockwell was his name, and he managed to find us a cabin. 3:30, here comes Alice, my mother, and the two boys. We get to stay in this little shack, all of us.

My mother and Alice got jobs in the cannery as slimers for that summer. When it came to the end of the season, we went into Juneau and she sent the two boys back down to their father in San Diego. We came out to Angoon with the fish buyer Tommy Gregory, a good friend of mine. I had a beat up old skiff called the "No Hope"; it was plywood and leaked and everything. Alice's first visit to Angoon, we came up on the fish buyer up in Kootznoowoo Inlet, and I got her in my skiff and we were coming around over here by the graveyard, and she was sitting on the gas tank. The skiff was plywood and a kind of little groove in the inside hull, and water was not bad, but water was leaking into the boat. So I said "I'll drop you off over here and I'll pick you up on the other side of the graveyard". I figured if I got her out of the boat, it wouldn't leak. I tell her there's a trail; it's just a few hundred yards around to the other side of the point. She goes, and I hear her screaming, she's screaming on the trail. I yell, "What's the matter?" And she says, "I'm falling in graves!" There's old graves down there, and they've sunk down, some of them pretty deep, and she's in all these berry bushes! This is her first trip to Angoon! So anyway, I picked her up on the other side, and we came in... She stayed with me for 44 years. Four children - three boys and a girl.

***

That's the reason I wish I could write a good poem for her. That woman adored me. That woman... loved me. I could do anything... just unbelievable. And we were together and had four kids, one drowned over in Sitka, Mark, and went to the end. 44 years. The perfect wife for me.

That's the guilt. She was unbelievable. I couldn't take a bossy woman, even today. I admit it.

***

Once I got back in Angoon, I was a hand troller. Never made much, you know. I'd go out here in front of the village; there were a lot of kings in those days, a lot of fish... but no price. Right here, around Danger Point. And we rowed. We didn't have out-board motors in those days. We rowed all day, trolling. First we lived in a tent, up the trail where my son is buried now. Then we built a little shack, dad helped build it, 12x16. Then we started having babies. And then one day there's a knock on the door, and here's a guy in a suit in my little shack. He says, "I'm with the federal government Indian Relocation Program.", and he came in and we talked about it, and he said "If you were to get a job or an occupation, what would it be?" I said, "Well, I think I'd like to be a teletype mechanic because I was a teletype operator in the Air Force, and if I could get the mechanics I could get a remote spot and be an operator and a repairman." So anyway, he set it up and he sent my whole family to Oakland, California, and I went through electronics school building radios, TVs, radios: Radio/Electronics/Television School. He got me a job through the Indian Relocation Program; they paid for the whole thing, and we managed to get enough money to buy a brand new car for $2,600, a Comet, and we drove up.

I had a job arranged in Anchorage as an electrician, and I didn't like it. It's all mathematical. You can figure out any electrical problem through mathematics. Anyway, after we got up to Tok or Haines Junction, I said, "You know, Alice, Southeast has always been good to me." I didn't like electronics anyway. So we turned and came back to Southeast. And as usual I did a little fishing, never made much money, but we could eat a lot of clams off the beach. Rice. Macaroni and cheese, only $0.25 a box. We packed our water from here up to the cabin.

***

The state had a list, from A to Z, for different kinds of jobs that the state offers. You can get on these lists - you read what the qualifications are, and I fit about 20 of them. One of them was a boat officer. The first year, around 1954, I worked for employment security claims, $350 a month. We lived in Cedar Park in Juneau, a low rent place. We came back here to Angoon the next summer, fished. We went back to Juneau the next year, and they said we have a better position for you, we're going to make you Clerk III. So then I was in the administration section. During that time I also ran a multilith printing machine. I ran all the budgets and documents for the state. I didn't like it. I was down in the basement, and we used all these chemicals cleaning the press and all that. I'd come back to Angoon to fish, and then I'd go back to that. I'd work doing Christmas packages, anything to fill in. While I was there as a multilith operator, they said that they'd just hired a boat officer in Sitka who was a non-resident, when they should have hired me as a resident on the employment list. They were watching out for me and he had to take me. They made him fire the guy, and I went over and became a boat captain for Fish & Game. I ran the Skip Jack out of Sitka, and later ran all the boats for Fish & Game. I did that for a while, and then in 1966 they asked how I'd like to be a Protection Officer in Petersburg. They'd just fired somebody. I said sure, so I went down to Petersburg, and everybody loved me down there too, by the way. They loved me everywhere. So I worked Petersburg for 5 years. Got friends. I thought everybody hated me because I cited everybody in town. They promoted me to Sergeant - I was going to Ketchikan. As I was leaving, out at the ferry terminal lot, about 300 people showed up - they said, "You're a real asshole, but you're real fair. You treated everybody the same."

And so I went to Ketchikan, worked down there 5 years, and then they promoted me to a Lieutenant, and then they transferred me out of Ketchikan. I made some major cases, including one involving the United States and Canada where the boundary line is. I arrested - took a boat hostage down there. I saw in the Alaska history - and it's wrong in there - that the boat took me to Prince Rupert, forced me. They didn't. I was on the boat, and I told them they were fishing in American waters. This is where the line is, between Canada and the United States, at Point Chacon. They claim their line goes right to Cape Chacon, and we claim 3 miles out from Cape Chacon. The governor had sent orders already that we enforce that 3-mile territorial line.

I was out, I was in Ketchikan, 1973 maybe. Alice and her sister and son had come up, and we were out sport fishing in Carroll Inlet, about 6 miles from Ketchikan. This plane kept circling around, finally landed, and they said they want me out in Cape Chacon. Some Fish & Game boat had reported this Canadian boat fishing. I was in hip boots; I had my family on board the boat in the inlet. I jumped on the airplane and said I'd be back in about an hour. So anyway, I took off on the airplane, and I got out there, and they showed me the boat. Sure enough, it was in American waters. The pilot told me that he could land, but wouldn't be able to take off again. I said, "No, over on the shore by Cape Chacon there are some bays with some tenders in them. Take me over to one of those tenders." So he landed, and I commanded one of the tenders to take me out to the boat. He didn't want to, but he had to. I got out and told him he wouldn't have to stay, that I'd just jump aboard when we got there. We get out there and there's one old man and two boys, and they've been fishing halibut. They're all pooped out, and I could have taken all three of them on at the same time. But before I got off the plane, I told them to get a hold of the Fish and Game boat that reported it, about 20 miles away, and have them send down NOAA aides in a skiff. This is a true story, it didn't come out this way; Ottawa changed the whole thing.

So I get on the fishing boat, and I tell them, "I want you -", I didn't say they're under arrest, "I want you to go back to Ketchikan." And he kept showing me the charts, you know, "No, I'm

19

in Canadian waters.", "No, you're in American waters.", on and on. "Can I call my company?" I say, "Yeah, call your company". And they say, "Put the officer off, and return. Leave the gear and return." And he said, "I can't, there's no way here to drop him off." About that time, the skiff arrives, the boat I called to come. And there's a guy named Noah, a bouncer, no brains whatsoever, but physical. And he was in there and he came up and I said, "Stay off" - true story, though it's not written this way - I said "If this boat's going back to Prince Rupert, I'm going with it". We got going, they'd been up 3, 4 nights in a row. This is a real old man, a couple heart attacks already, and a couple young kids, they were all tired. And he says, "Do you have any experience running a boat? Know how to run a course?" I said yeah, I was a boat skipper for Fish & Game. They went to bed and I ran the boat back to Prince Rupert! We get to Prince Rupert, and I'm still in my hip boots and jeans from sport fishing with my family. They kept me down there three days interviewing me and all that sort of thing. It went clear back to Ottawa, their government, that I was a pirate and all that sort of thing. Finally on the third day they flew me back to Ketchikan. I got a letter from Governor Egan saying what a good job I did. But if you read the articles now, it says I ordered them, arrested them, they ran back with me, captured me, took me back. I say, "You don't know Sharp. Nobody is going to kidnap Sharp. Nobody." I was at the wheel!

***

It was a wonderful time to be working in Alaska. This was all untouched. No logging, no nothing. The gang in Petersburg, they're all dead now. Harry Mariam was in charge of the Game Division, and Norm Johnson was in charge of Commercial Fish. Norm hated protection officers because he didn't think they were doing their job. The first thing I did was I caught the biggest creek robber in Southeast Alaska, got him convicted. When I came back to my office, there was a bottle of whisky on the table. I won Norm Johnson over. He hated protection officers.

The fisherman was Bill Love. He'd been cited many times but never convicted. That's the reason Norm Johnson gave me the whisky. We had stakeout teams. I had about 30 stakeout teams per summer, 2 guys. We'd take them out and put them in closed waters and teach them how to kayak in the Klepper type kayaks. They had to put them together and take them apart within so many minutes. We had training classes which I taught in Pybus Bay. They weren't allowed to leave any sign, they had to hide their camp, they had to stay out of sight. And then they'd watch creeks. We had lots of them. One fisherman told me, "Christ, Frank, you have somebody out in every bay!" And I said, "Hey, if you have that opinion, I'm doing my job."

Anyway, it was Red Bluff Bay. I had two really good guys from Wyoming staked out there. Red Bluff Bay is a big bay that goes in and then narrows down to a little pass and then it opens up again in the back. It's all closed to fishing back there. They were out on this hill, and Bill Love came in and made his set, and the team is playing cards on a log. Bill said later that the fish pulled him in, 20,000 or something fish in the seine. His defense was that they were all swimming, even though the tide was going out, and they all swam and pulled him into the bay. And he said it was windy, and the boys said, "No, it wasn't windy, we were playing cards on a log!". So anyway, we got a conviction. And then I caught him again, caught him a second time. Ended his career as a seiner. But he appealed. Way later, I came to find out that his girlfriend was on the jury, and they cleared him of that robbery. But he never seined again. I caught him twice.
***

Harry Mariam, in charge of the Game Division always sat in the office, never went anywhere, but he was the one saying how many deer there were, how many bear there were. All he would do is run Wrangell Narrows, basically. I'd get in my Bertram, I'd run up here, all around Baranof, Chichagof (Islands), always in the Bertram. I'd say, "Hey, I saw 243 deer here, I saw this in this bay, this in that." His report would just be what he saw in Wrangell Narrows. My whole career, there's not one evaluation up there that's not outstanding or better. Not one. I'll tell you why.

When someone committed a Fish & Game crime in my area, they weren't doing it to the state. I was responsible for that area and they were doing it to me. And I'm out there on weekends, I'm out there all the time. Even with my family.

But I was fair, and I'll give you an example. There's a little creek, Stink Creek, across from Petersburg. It's got fish. I see a skiff - this is right across from Petersburg - and I know that somebody's fishing. So I walk in and I can't find the trail, exactly, but I look up and I see a fishing pole and an arm. I don't see a person. They must have seen me or heard me or something. Because after a little while, I see where the trail is, I start up the trail, and here they come down. No gear, nothing. And I ask if there's anybody else, and they say no, nobody there. The skiff had gone dry down at the beach, and I offered to help them, and I asked them if they're sure they didn't see anybody. So I went with my aide back up to the lake, knowing that they had to have hid their gear. And it's all wild, and I see a scuff on a log. Sure enough, underneath, a fishing pole, the whole thing. So I wrote them a note, saying if you want your gear come to my office on Monday morning. He came in to get his gear. I said, "Tell you what. I never really saw you. All I saw is an arm and a fishing pole.", and I gave him back the gear. Do you know what kind of guts it took for him to come into the office? That's the way I always was. I tried to be fair.

***

If you're going to do a job, you do it good. You give it everything you have. When you're running a mile, you put on a big push at the end. That's the way I always was. I was responsible. That was me. That was my area. If I went upstairs and got all of my evaluations from boat officer onwards, you can see, this guy is tremendous. It just happened that way. I was an officer in Petersburg, and then they sent me to Ketchikan to be a Sergeant. I was there five years, and they transferred me to Anchorage as a Lieutenant. And then they say they're making me in charge of all the waters of Alaska, as a Captain. Coastal Commander, in charge of all the waters of Alaska clear up to the Arctic. Ketchikan up, the whole thing.

***

They would send me North. The Bertram story is a good example. They would send me up to Bristol Bay every year to work. We had Boston Whalers that we'd use to run the fishery up there, opens early in July. We'd be there and then we'd run around, it was a nightmare up there, so many boats making sets all over. One time I was down in Petersburg and my boss calls me, Buck Stewart, he died last year. He says, "Frank, I want you to run the Bertram to Bristol Bay." I said, "Well, I'm going out to Kake to pick up a cub black bear", and he said, "No, how soon can you go to Bristol Bay?" I told him I could go that afternoon. I went out to get bananas and pork and beans and fueled up with a spare drum, and took off. I ran up to Angoon and stopped to visit my dad for a little bit, then I ran up to Yakutat, Seward,

Kodiak, Sand Point, to fuel up, and then through False Pass, and delivered the boat up to King Salmon. Alone. 2600 miles. 20 days, as I remember. I didn't have navigational stuff, and there are big sandbars off the coast, way off the coast. I'd sit out on the flying bridge, and wait for the water to change color. I went by the color of the water. Several times I had to retract and go out a little further. Just another job to do. Buck Stewart, he came down for my best friend Wayne Fleek's wedding, nine years ago or so. We were riding in the car, and he said "Frank? Sorry I sent you to Bristol Bay."

Now, if I could arrange it, I want to run my 15-foot Pacific Mariner to Hawaii. I really do. If I could get fuel, because I can't carry enough for the long way, I'd go to Hawaii in my Pacific Mariner right now. That's how much I trust that boat. It wouldn't sink.

Frank Sharp's home in Angoon, Alaska

Frank Sharp, Angoon, Alaska 2017

Work & Duty

Mr. President

Oh! Mr. President young m
Why must our young m
can't you tell us why
Daddy wont be home to
He's been made a prisoner
He says not to worry ti
Couldn't love us more
Oh! Mr. President
Why must our young men
Oh! Mr. D........ why?
can't you won't ne tonight
Daddy wont ever more
e will he died in that prison c
te victim of Nixons war
I Mr. President
y must our young men di
Mr. President
you tell us why?

Daddy Won't Be Home Tonight

Daddy won't be home tonight He's busy fighting wars

Nations far across the seas

Trying to destroy our democracy

Oh! Mr. President
Why must our young men die? Oh! Mr. President
Can't you tell us why?

Daddy won't be home tonight He's been made a prisoner of war

He says not to worry

And that he couldn't love us more

Oh! Mr. President Can't you tell us why?
Daddy won't be home tonight Nor will he ever-
more
He died in that prison camp   A victim of a useless war

Oh! Mr. President
Why must our young men die Oh Mr. President

Can't you tell us why?

Kill the
In the land of Viet...
On the steamy jungle front
Sure of his skill
Doubt deep in his mind endured
Would he be able to kill

For it seemed like yesterday
In the comfort of his home
He was just the kid with a car
Always on the phone
Cars and girls and who's at bat
His most serious decisions
Now here he was alone
A member of marine Division

On that fatal foggy morn
Caught in the foggy swirl
He saw his first enemy
And that she was a girl
Twelve weeks of combat t...
A lifetime of right does n...
And in his hesitation to
This young lad dies

He was a tallish lad
Barely out of his teens

He Was A Tallish Lad

He was a tallish lad
Barely out of his teens
When he received his orders
To replace by uniform his jeans

On the steamy jungle front
Sure of his skill
Doubt deep inside endured
Would he be able to kill?

For it seemed like yesterday
In the comfort of his home
He was just a kid with acne
Always on the phone

Cars, girls, and who's at bat
His most serious decisions
Now here he was alone
A member of Marine Divisions

On that last and fatal morn
There caught in a foggy swirl
He saw his first enemy
And that she was a girl

Twelve weeks of combat training
A lifetime of right does not comprise
In his hesitation to kill
This young lad dies

He was a tallish lad
Barely out of his teens
When to rest they laid him
Replaced by uniform, his jeans

AS THE YOUTH'S OF TODAY

WE ARE THE ADULTS

OF TOMORROW

WE KNOW NOT WHAT

THE FUTURE HOLDS

IN SWAY

OR WHETHER THE PATHS

WE FOLLOW ARE PITTED

WITH HAPPY TIMES

OR ~~MANY~~ SORROW'S

IN TH[...]IAD OF

OUR LIFE'S [...]S

BUT [...] YOUTH

FILLS US WITH ENTHUSIA[...]

FOR WHATEVER LIES

AHEAD ~~OF US~~

~~OUR YOUTH~~

~~BUT~~ WE WILL

LIE IN
MAKE OUR OWN B[...]

AND PACE THE, F[...]

AS YOUR GENERATION[...]

Youth of Today (for the class of '89)

As the youths of today
We are the adults
of tomorrow

We know not what
the future holds
in sway

Or whether the paths
We follow are pitted
With happy times
Or sorrows
In the myriad of
Our life's days

But our youth
fills us with enthusiasm
for whatever lies ahead
We will
Lie in our own bed

To face the future
As your generations did
We cannot always do your Bid

We'll make our mistakes
We'll have to eat our own Cake
As you did

Adversity will make us strong
It will put us where we belong
We seek your advice
We know you care
But don't be too restrictive
Or vindictive
When we don't respond

For we must dare

G7   C

... ... my ... ... is rich in the North land

C   G7   C

... ... a   Soaking up the

G7

... a ... the sea ... way appealed

... in ... ... Out on the pipe

G7

... my memories of my trip - down to

F G7 C

... When the nights are six months long.

Working on the Pipeline

Working on the pipeline,
In Alaska!
Seven twelves is my shift,
Gettin' rich in the Northland
Then I'm gonna drift

Tallahassee, Miami, Houston & LA,
Soakin' up the sunshine,
But I ain't gonna stay...

I'm going to take a trip,
Across the sea,
Hong Kong has always appealed
to me...

And when the seasons,
Turn to fall,
I'll be back in that
Union Hall!

Out on the pipeline
temperature 60 below...
I'll have my memories
Of my trip
Down below...

Readin' my Playboy,
Can you blame me boy?
When the nights are six months long.

... A BY T... ...TERS

... LAW ENFORCEMENT
... ACADEMY

... ...
... ...TS BEAR THE STRA...
FROM PHYSICAL FITNESS PROGRA...
... ... OF THE BRAIN

FROM SEARCH AND SIEZURE
AND RULES OF EVIDENCE
TO SWIMMING, BASKETBALL
AND THE ART OF SELF DEFENSE

DAILY INSPECTIONS, BY THE STA...
ARE THE GENERAL RULE
WHEN EIGHT O... ROLLS ROUN...
BETTER NOT ... FOR SCHOOL

SHINE THAT ...
DUST THAT S...
HEY YOU TROOPER
DUMP THAT TRASH

YES SIR! AND NO SIR!
ECHO THROUGH THE HALLS
AND AT NIGHT YOU WILL FIND ...
THESE RECRUITS, WASHING DOWN T...

...HEN THE DAY IS THROUGH
...D ABOUT TO START THE NEXT
...'S TIME TO OPEN THAT BOOK
...D READ THAT INTERESTING TEXT

CAP A...

Ode to the Academy

They make State Troopers
At Sitka by the sea
Trained in law enforcement
At the Academy

From dawn to dusk,
These recruits bear the strain
From physical fitness
To developing of the brain

From search and seizure
And rules of evidence
To swimming, basketball
And the art of self defense

Daily inspections, by the staff
Are the general rule
When eight o'clock rolls round
Better not be late for school

Shine that floor
Dust that sash
Hey you trooper
Dump that trash

Yes sir! No sir!
Echo through the halls
And at night you will find
These recruits, washing walls

When the day is through
And about to start the next
It's time to open that book
And read that interesting text

If car A struck car B
And left sixty feet of track
Use your nomograph stupid
And get off my aching back

But the final day
Will be well worth the while
When they call you trooper
And you don't have to run the mile!!

CLEAR TO THE BOTTOM $2.00

THERE IS NOT A LOT
THEY HAVE NO VALUE

NO DIVIDENDS DO I S
ONLY DISBURSEMENTS THAT

IVE GOT THE FORZOOUBOU I
CLEAR TO BOTTOM OF
COMPANY ENTS AL
WERE ON OUR WAY TO BANKS

AND FOR OUR PEOPLE THAT
T OFTEN PROMISES WRITT
ABE OF TISSUE

CAN nHAVE LAND THE
T YOU CAN ONLY
nDO IT

Kootznoowoo Inc. Blues

I've got the Kootznoowoo Inc. blues
Clear to the bottom of my rubber shoes.

Though I've got a lot of stock
They have no value on the block
No dividends do I see
Only disbursements that break the company

I've got the Kootznoowoo Inc blues
Clear to the bottom of my rubber shoes

Company investments all so poor
We're on our way to bankruptcy, that's for sure
Land for our people, that's the issue
But often promises are written on paper made of tissue

You can have land they say
But you can only do it our way!

99 year leases, so you can't mortgage or sell
But that doesn't apply to Kootznoowoo as well
They will sell the land to cover corporation expenses
No lease restrictions apply to others
Only to us sisters and brothers

So come on my corporation
We still have faith in you
We know you all know what to do
It's still not too late
Open the gate and go through

You have our affection
Now's the time
To change direction
The dream of a good life can come true

Seven!
They were seven
considering, debating the law
of the land.
Adoption, rejection.
That was thier plan.
They stood tall, in thier decisio
Down to the seventh man
Many were hardship ri
In playing roles,
No matter .... ___ is e thier ju
The public defamed them
Down to the Seventh man
Volunteer all, still they stay
Refusing to falter from thier
Protect Alaska' resocrees, Down
To prowite benefits for all

Down to the Seventh Man

Seven!
They were seven
Considering, debating the laws
Of the land.
Adoption, rejection,
That was their plan.
They stood tall, in their decisions,
Down to the seventh man.
Many were their hardships,
In playing their roles.
No matter how wise their judgements ran,
The public defamed them,
Down to the seventh man.
Volunteer all, still they stayed,
Refusing to falter from their original plan.
Protect Alaska resources, down to the seventh man.
To provide benefits for all,
Their only reward, these men of the Fisheries
Board!
A meritorious goal!
Call the roll...
Szabo, Beaton, Goll, Fair, Jenson, Huntington,
Schroeder.
Down to the seventh man.

Adventure

HADN'T I SEEN EM ALL [BUT FAZE MC]
THE BIG AND THE SMALL?
NOTHING, COULD A MAZE ME

SO I NONCHALANTLY CRANKED
LIKE ALL OF THE HUNDREDS OF
AND IT WASN'T UNTIL I SAW H.
I KNEW THIS FISH, WASN'T
LIKE HIS OTHER SISTERS AND BROTH
HERE WAS A FISH, THAT WAS A
LIKE NONE EVER BEFORE SEEN
A FISHERMANS DREAM!
HANGING TH   MY HOOK
A FISH FOR   CORD BOOK
THEN I BEG   TO SHIVER
MY BROW RAN WET WITH S
FOR I S-DOENLY REALIZED
I COULDN'T KEEP THIS PRIZE
FOR THE SEASON ON KING SAC
HADN'T OPENED YET!
WAS I TO BE DENIED?
-ORD WHY NOW I CRIED!
I BEGAN TO PLOT AND PLAN
-IKE ANY

A Fishtale

When that fish took the hook it didn't even faze me.
For hadn't I seen them all, the large and the small?
Nothing would amaze me. So I nonchalantly cranked him in,
Like all the hundreds of others, and it wasn't till I saw this fish,
I knew he wasn't anything like his other sisters and brothers.
Here was a Fish that was a Fish! A fisherman's dream!
Hanging there on my hook, a fish for the record book!

I began to tremble, my brow ran wet with sweat
For, suddenly, I realized, I couldn't keep this prize,
For the season on Chinook hadn't opened yet.
Why now, Lord, I cried, was I the record to be denied?
So, like any man, I began to plot and plan
How I'd kill this fish and hide him away,
And later, if asked, I'd say, with a leer,
That I had caught this fish on sports gear,
That would be regal, for then this fish would be legal!
But alas, it came to pass my conscience came to fore,
I knew I couldn't kill this Fish,
For even that I would abhor. For you most all know,
A warden I was, am and always will be. So, I set that fish free.

But what of my bragging rights on those long winter nights?
Of this silver monster I'd plucked from the Arctic sea?
Who'd believe me?
Another tale they'll say, of the whale that got away,
A whale that got bigger in the telling, each day.

To make thing's worse, I am doubly cursed, for who'd believe,
if my tale is so, that I would let such a fish go?
Between you and my maker, I swear, my tale is true,
well knowing that forever, I'll never get my due.
To my principles however, I stayed true!

SINGIGRACHACK ON

Take me back
To Singigrachack
on that old chukchi sea

I long _____ life
on the _____ .ak
That _____ so much t

Oh how I wish
That I again
could fish

on those northern
where nets are
In the tidal bor

Singigrachack on the Chukchi Sea

Take me back
To Singigrachack
On that old Chukchi Sea

I long for that life
on the Noatak
That meant so much to me

Oh how I wish
That I again
could fish

On those Northern shores
where nets are set
in the tidal bores

The fishing nets
And drying racks, quickly
filling with the silvery hordes

myluvin old
all
noueuralon

me achargin
reth agleamin white
I froze where I stood
verin in shame RUL fright

's bear
ts breath ot seal astinkin
I my miserable
utendin to in athink
set my fro

shoot man
or your guts will be aflap
what of your plows dou
After this scason atr

So intent on my hid
This bear cleanly m
me alyin there
nkin sure

The Look On That Bear's Face

It came a'chargin'
Its teeth a'gleamin' white
and I froze where I stood
A'shiverin' in shameful fright

This bear
Its breath of seal a'stinkin'
Intendin' to end my miserable life
Set my frozen brain a'thinkin'

Shoot, man, shoot!
Or your guts will be a'flappin'
what of your plans down below
After this season a'trappin?

So intent on my hide a'eatin
This bear clearly missed the jump,
Me a'lyin' there a'gapin'
A'thinkin' sure I was sunk

He turned
And with a look that astounded
He smiled I'm sure
Before over the hill he bounded.

Oft when I'm a'drinkin'
Or a'restin' in in my shack
With the wind in the trees a'howlin'
The look on that bear's face comes back.

Wiley Black rolled a
y, he was headed for the spot
r each and every year
him had been a deer Cattle

dream, still with no luck,
ve point buck!

n skilled hunters pride,
knew, deep inside,
y, he'd nail that monsters h

n, just past noon,
sun, shin___ ___ his fac
approached ___t special
he blew t___ ___coning
rh loving grace ___ ___all,
saw, in steael of a de
Beam in its place.

a blink of the eye
t Bear was at his fe

question now was t
that Bear to die?
___ his strength

Encounter of a Different Kind

All week he had stalked,
The wily black tailed deer,
Today, he was headed for the spot,
That each and every year
For him, had been a deer cattle lot.

His dream, still with no luck,
A five-point buck!
With skilled hunter's pride,
He knew, deep inside, today,
He'd nail that monster's hide.

Soon, just past noon,
The sun shining in his face,
He cautiously approached,
His special place.

As he blew that beckoning call,
With loving grace,
He saw, instead of a deer,
A bear in its place!

With a roar and bounding leap,
That bear made straight for Fleek!
In the blink of an eye,
That bear was at his feet.

The question now was,
He or that bear to die?

With all his strength,
At rifle barrel's length,
He fired from the hip,
The bear flipped, into the air,
Knocking Fleek down,

Now the pair, he and the bear,
Lay motionless on the soggy
ground.

Then, silence... not a sound!

When Fleek stood up,
To consider his luck,
The bear lay dead on the ground.

He knew he'd looked fate,
in the face, squarely,
And thank God he'd escaped,
bearily,
An encounter of a different kind.

... ...

as many times in the
world in our desire t
well knowing this journ
___

This journey to be our
mortal man would ne
And when he heard w
this understanding to a
___

he seas w [i]olent
nd my friend strained
answers had had thier
aths reaper by even
___

r we knew our des
trip for weeks we
night with the dev

March 15th, 1966: Peril Strait

We left at dawn,
This friend and me,
As many times in the past,
United in our desire to be free,
Well knowing this journey to be our last

This journey to be our greatest venture,
Mortal man would never understand
And when he heard would censure,
This undertaking to a forbidden land

The wilds and seas were violent this morning,
And my friend strained to stay afloat,
Mariners had had their warning,
Death's reaper by evening would gloat

For we knew our destination well,
A trip for weeks we'd planned,
Tonight with the devil we'd walk,
By the flames of Hades fanned.

OH LISTEN TO THE
AS ~~THE THAT~~ AIRPLANE
THAT TALKEETNA R
THE CHUGACH
STAND MAJESTIC
AND IM FILLED WI
AT TV   IAGNIF
THE TA   HITE BI
FALL C   STRA
ME WHY I LOVE
WHERE GIANT MOOSE
ABOUND AND FLOW
MILLIONS GLOW UPON
GROUND——

FRAN

Talkeetna River Shore

Listen to the rumble,
Listen to the roar,
As that Airplane carries me,
To that Talkeetna River shore.

The Chugach Mountains,
Stand majestically to my right,
And I am filled with wonder,
At this magnificent sight.

The tall white Birch,
In their Fall colors stand,
Reassuring me of why,
I Love this Alaska Land.

Where giant moose,
And Caribou abound,
And Flowers by the millions,
Grow upon the Tundra Ground.

My Pilot signals,
We are about to land,
As he skillfully sets Piper 24 Zulu,
Softly, upon the River's sand.

This is the Talkeetna River Camp,
On the Talkeetna River Shore,
Where there are thrills for all,
In store.

Where Nature's wonders,
Are all collected,
And Peace
Is truly found,
In the rustling of
Fall leaves,
Amid the clustered trees,
And in the myriad,
Of nature's many sights
and sounds

Where friendships,
Over coffee strengthen,
And tales,
Before a fire are told,
As evenings,
Dark shadows, lengthen,
And fire's ashes grow cold.

Oh! Listen to the rumble,
Listen to the roar,
As that Talkeetna River,
Winds its way, back,
To that Cook Inlet Shore.

I've sailed on stormy waters
Flown ~~alone~~ in a sunset sky
Felt the exuberance of victory
The chill of one about to die.
I've made love to a virgin woman
Shared in her spasmic sighs,
Dove to the ocean depths
climbed the highest peaks
Stood on the Mohave desert, 2
Dined with ... chiefs,
I've been ... A sailor,
killed my ...
Sought f...
Through religion, Drugs
Every way you can
I've ~~felt~~ the eagerness of
The frustration of the m
I've laughed a million laug
Shed a million tears
But before it is all ove
There ~~are a lot of~~ thin

Do It All

I've sailed on troubled waters
Flown alone in a sunset sky
Felt the exuberance of victory
The chill of one about to die.
I've made love to many women
Shared in their spasmic sighs.
Dove to the ocean depths
Climbed the highest peaks
Stood on the Mohave Desert
I've dined with Indian chiefs
I've been a soldier, a sailor,
Killed my fellow man
Sought peace
through religion, drugs
Every way you can
I've felt the eagerness of youth
The frustration of the middle years
I've laughed a million laughs
Shed a million tears
But before it is all over and through
There are things I still would like to do
take a spaceship to the stars
visit Pluto, the moon, Mars
Walk the length of the China wall
Tour the Taj Mahal
Yes,
Do it all.

TO GUIDE OUR
FOLLOW ME!
OUR FELLOW MAD
THERE'S A SAFE H
JUST AHEAD

HIS LIGHT,
OUR ONLY BEAC
SHOWING THE
TO THE SAFETY
IN A SHELTER B
FOLLOW THE LIGHT
UR SAVIOR SAI
HE WINDS AND
RE AWFULLY RO
ND KEEP

Steamer Bay

The winds not steady
But of roaring gusts
Caught the churning seas
And threw them at us

Our sturdy little ship
Strained to stay afloat
As the night's deep darkness
Surrounded our pitching boat

Our crew
three men of different breed
Although together were alone
Each with a separate need

Hal from Boston
An attorney by trade
Later admitted
His thoughts were of Susan
And vows they had made

And Stan
The Nebraska Man
Tended to chores to be done
Well knowing he'd never see
the morning sun

And I
The experienced Alaska mate
Thought only of saving my ship
From the grip of nature's fate

And out of the darkness
A call for help went
And soon
An answer sent

Hold on!
Don't give up hope
Fight those winds and seas
Try to stay afloat

And soon a light appeared
To guide our way
Follow me! Our fellow mariner said
There's a safe harbor just ahead

His light our only beacon
Showing the way
To the safety we were seeking
In a sheltered bay

Follow the light our savior said
The winds and seas are awfully rough
And keeping steady course
For me is especially tough

I've got to go
These winds are wailing
You will be safe here I know
And from here on, good sailing!

...ience this information gave m...
...e for being rescued as I knew t...
...w if they knew where I was...
...sea conditions, visibility op...
...would have to cover just...
...the area which covered thous...
...me miles there was little o...
...would find me in time

As I stood there close on
the Bertram I decided that I...
...t to die n...
...he water I... on my
...when the...
...below the... decided
...ould strap c... 358 revo...
...t the last moment whi...
...t was going under I wo...
...y self Not wanting the ay...
...wing, I strapped on my Gu...

During this time there...
...tearly clean radio squeal fr...
...rescuers say the cutter is...
...close. A C 130 Aircraft is...
...ay from Kodiak. Keep Calm...

Bertram 3

"Mayday! Mayday! Mayday! This is the Bertram 3. Does anyone read me?"

I screamed over and over into my marine radio, hearing only silence.

"Mayday! Mayday! Mayday! This is the Bertram 3 Does anyone read me?" Over and over.

I was somewhere off the mouth of the Copper River, caught in heavy wind and seas. I was trying desperately to stay afloat in my 25 ft Bertram Day Cruiser, the two engines still running. I would head the boat into the giant white capped seas that continuously crashed down on my small craft. On the downside of the waves I would cut the throttle fully back as I literally tumbled down the side of the 30 foot waves thinking that at the bottom my boat would capsize and the next wave would bury me and my boat.

Valiantly, the Bertram would miraculously climb back up the next mountainous wave and slide down the backside.

"Mayday, Mayday, Mayday!", I screamed. Suddenly, on the downside of a wave, the sea crashed down on me and my craft with the might of a tidal wave. My craft shuddered, tossed, and pitched violently as the seas filled the boat. I was trapped inside as I fought to open the jammed bulkhead door that separated the small cabin from the back deck. I kicked at the bulkhead door, desperately trying to gain access to the back deck.

All I had aboard was a life preserver and my lifeboat - if you wanted to call it that. It was an 8ft plastic tub shaped craft called a 'Sport Yak' which, as any mariner knows, is barely safe to row ashore in a calm harbor. Forunately, the seawater that had filled the Bertram drained down into the lower hull, leaving the top dry. I now had no power, as the seawater had filled the engine room and batteries.

The seas as violent as ever, now seemed serene, my boat now just a piece of flotsam on the giant ocean, floating like a cork upon the waves. Up and down, up and down, up and down we crashed, as I stood on the back deck, tense but with no real feeling of fear.

First I prayed: 'Lord, many times in the past when death was near, I asked that you save me and I promised that if you would save me from my peril, I would become a better person. We both know that I never kept those promises. So I'm not going to make any promises to you now. If you are going to take me you are going to have to take me just the way I am.

Then suddenly, a miracle occurred! Through the radio, battered and covered by seawater, which had been silent till then, I heard a very faint voice which seemed to be responding to my calls for help.

I asked, "Are you answering the Bertram 3?"

Very weakly, I heard the voice say, "Roger, Roger, Roger."

Someone in Kodiak had heard my plea for help.

Miraculously, my radio received clear contact with people in Cordova and the U.S Coast Guard. Though the wind and seas continued unabated, tossing me and my boat like clothes in a dryer, this connection with the outside world made me feel that I wasn't alone. However, with my experience as a boatman I knew there was little chance for me to be rescued. I didn't know where I was, there was little or no visibility, and the seas continued their unabated crashing and smashing upon us.

Late afternoon was approaching, and soon it would be dark. I knew I could never survive the night. I felt calm through it all. Yes, I cried! I guess I was afraid, but not of death.

I radioed: "Tell my wife I love her and that it's been a good life! I'm not afraid of death because I believe."

Potential rescuers radioed telling me to stay calm, that they were sending a Coast Guard cutter out of Cordova and a C-130 out of Kodiak to search for me. Because of my marine experience, this information gave me little hope of being rescued as I knew that even if they knew where I was located, the sea conditions, visibility, approaching dark, and distance left little or no chance they would locate me in time.

As I stood there alone on the back deck, I decided that I did not want to die fighting for my last breath. If and when the Bertram sunk below the seas, I decided that I would strap on my 358 revolver and at the last moment while the boat was going down I would shoot myself to avoid the agony of drowning.

During this time there was a steady clear radio signal from my rescuers. "The cutter is leaving Cordova. A C-130 aircraft is on its way from Kodiak." I was told that my best friend was out flying his aircraft regardless of flying conditions, futilely searching for me as best he could.

I knew a C-130 Coast Guard rescue aircraft was now in the area searching for me, but visibility was less than half a mile. The seas on top of the waves were crashing frothy white. The Bertram was all white from top to bottom, and from the air it would be nearly impossible to distinguish from the white caps of the frothing seas.

And then a radio message from the C-130, "Sorry partner, but we have to return to base; our navigational radar has failed."

Hearing that, I lost my last hope of rescue. I stood there numbed by the situation when, suddenly, the C-130 appeared directly above me. I desperately called on the radio, "You're right over me! You're right over me!"

Circling above me for hours, often losing sight of me, I would call them, "Come right! Come left!", holding on to my only chance at survival. The C-130 had again radioed Kodiak for the Coast Guard rescue helicopters to head for the C-130's location in the high winds, estimated at 60 knots with 30 ft seas, making the flight slow and dangerous. Still, they continued on, and finally I heard and saw this angel in the sky which was to lift me up skyward to safety.

As the rescuers hovered above my swamped boat trying over and over again to set the rescue basket on my small pitching boat, they gave me instructions about how to enter the basket. I shouted, "Can I bring anything?" Back came the answer, "No!". Disregarding those instructions, I grabbed my stock issued Pentax camera and placed the strap over my neck. Remembering that I had bought my youngest son a Fonzi t-shirt before departing Seattle, I stuffed the t-shirt into my shirt.

Finally, the helicopter crew was able to set the rescue basket on the engine box of the Bertram. In the pitching seas, I grabbed on to the basket in a tight grip as the Coast Guard lifted the basket off the Bertram and I was swept under a giant wave. I remember opening my eyes and being underwater. Then momentarily I was above the wave in the trough; I quickly took a deep breath as I went under a second wave and then I was free of the sea.

The Coast Guard hoisted me aboard the helicopter, sat me down, and gave me a blanket. A few minutes later the crew chief came out of the cockpit and was cussing the lift crew. He came over to me and said, "Sorry partner, we are not supposed to troll you like that!" The Coast Guard flew me to Cordova.

I flew back to Anchorage to my wife and family, completed 20 years of state service, and retired. That was over 40 years ago.

Shortly after the incident, a friend sent me a wall plaque that he had carved showing a 25ft Bertram and this poem:

The Bertram is a boat of praise,
she stayed afloat through thunderous
waves - though swamped by seas
would not go down until her captain
was safe and sound - what greater
gift to one who loved her so then
grant him life to live his days
The Bertram is a boat of praise.

Bertram wall plaque and Frank Sharp

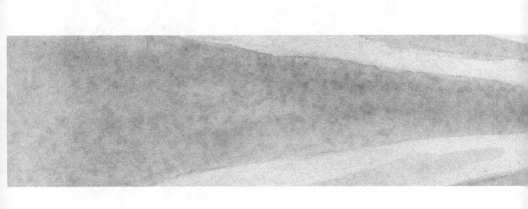

Love

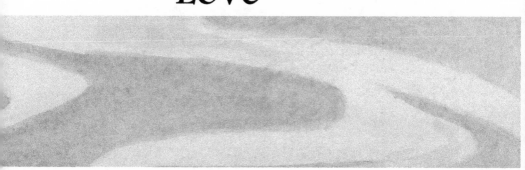

Onward down the track,
Watching out the window
Going forward, but thin

Thinking back to Hamil
Snow covered dales pas
I think of my Jeannie
And begin to cry

Begin to cry, though
Remembering the love
And me had

Moments d of te
That sweet smile or
Pierced my heart,
Like a warriors land

Here am i mortally
Not by gun or sword
Conquered by an ang
And i do thank the

Down the Track

Onward down the track,
Watching out the window,
Going forward, but thinking back

Thinking back to Hamilton,
Snow covered dales pass by,
I think of my Jeannie C,
And begin to cry

Begin to cry, though not sad,
Remembering the love we found,
And moments we had

Moments we had of tenderness,
That sweet smile or glance,
Pierced my heart,
Like a warrior's lance

Here am I mortally wounded,
Not by gun or sword,
Conquered by an angel,
And I do thank the Lord

Thank the Lord for living,
Making me good and clean,
Thank the Lord for giving,
Giving me life and Jean

Onward down the track,
Looking out the window,
Going forward,
But thinking back.

Tonight and all the

I am in love

spinning webs of

Like a spider far a

All the times weve

Theres one thing I

To tell you of you

And t love

Fate has turned aq

the clock even say

your face is ever.

Beautiful. even in

Now my eyes grow

And I hear the

Tonight and All the Nights Together

*In 1947-1948, I lived in Shawnee, Kansas with Mom
& Carl. I went to Center High in Kansas City, and
at school I became enamored with a little blonde girl
named Winnie Sue. My heart ached for Winnie Sue,
even though I don't think she knew I existed. One early
morning after having seen her at a school party and
having walked home 30 miles, I pined for Winnie Sue
and I wrote:*

Tonight
And all the nights together
I am in love
Spinning webs of daydreams
Like a spider, far above

The times we've been together
There's two things I forgot
To tell you
Of your great beauty
And that I love you
More than a lot

Fate has turned against me
The clock even speaks your name
Your face
Is everywhere
Beautiful even in the
Candle flame

Now,
My eyes grow heavy
And I hear the hoot owls beep
But I know I will still love you
When I have had some sleep

your eyes are like sunsh
radiating the warmth o
your lips so sweet-co
our two hearts are o

your laugh your smile
The smell of you
Drives me up that p
And like y dog-
To your beck
you are my s
when you are gone a
seeing

I shall fade as dusk
and die

your beauty Fu w

I love you more than

Your Eyes

*I've dedicated this poem to my wife Alice. My greatest regret is I never told her this while she was with me and now it's too late.

Your eyes
Are like sunshiny skies
Radiating the warmth
of the summer sun
Your lips, so sweet,
Communicating
That our two hearts
are one

Your laugh, your smile,
The scent of you
Drives me up
That proverbial wall
And like a puppy, I come
To your every beck and call
You are my life, my soul
my very being!

When you are gone and
No more I will be seeing
I shall fade as dusk to dark
and die
Your beauty in my heart.

I love you more than life itself
More than any other
A love above any other.

... for a happy ...
... at the same ...
THAT IS USUALLY FULL OF CHEER
AT THIS TIME OF YEAR AND OR...
OUR DAYS ARE DARK AND DR...
OUR HEARTS ARE ... AND ANOT...
FOR WE ARE WITHOUT THE O...
WHO BRIGHTENED OUR LIVES
THE ONE WHO TRIMMED THE T...
COOKED THE TURKEY
AND BAKED THE PUMPKIN P...
THE ONE WHO AT MIDNIGHT
PUT THE PRESENTS UNDER T...
WHILE EVERYONE WAS SLEEP...
AND COULD... E.

THE ONE ... WAS...
REALLY S... LAUS

FOR US TH... ...RRY
HAS BEEN TAKEN OUT OF
THE HAPPY
OUT OF NEW YEAR

AND FOREVER AFTER
CHRISTMAS WILL JUST
NEW YEAR JUST NEW
AND INSTEAD OF MERR...
A TIME TO SHED A T...

Christmas 2000

I know
You folks
Are completely sincere
In sending your Christmas greetings
And wishes for a happy new year
But at the Sharp house
That is usually full of cheer
At this time of year
Our days are dark and dreary
Our hearts are sad and weary
For we are without the one
Who brightened our lives
The one who trimmed the tree,
Cooked the turkey,
And baked the pumpkin pies
The one who at midnight
Put the presents under the tree
While everyone was sleeping
And couldn't see
The one who was...
Really Santa Claus
For us the merry
Has been taken out of Christmas
The happy
out of New Year
And forever after
Christmas will just be Christmas
New Year just New Year
And instead of merriment and cheer
A time to shed a tear.

...
...that precipitate
when I die I'd rather be planted
right here at home
For I've so enjoyed being busy eng...
Again holes of my own
Have given my sweat and tears
to this and these many years
why not my flesh and bone?
As my rotting flesh slowly decays
the earth sweetened
Like again
And where I nearby
New plants quickly grow
Their berries sweetened their flowe...
by my rotting overflow.
If in years hence
You come to visit or to resid...
And you see flowers blooming,
Sweet, ripe, berries by their sid...
You will know I am still among...
Not one of those who died.

Still Among the Living

If it weren't for my sweet lovin' old lady
Lying there in her grave all alone
Why, when I die
I would like to be planted
Right here at home
For I've so enjoyed
Being busily employed
Diggin holes of my own
Having given my sweat and tears
To these lands these many years
Why not my flesh and bone?

As my flesh decayed over time
The surrounding earth
Would be sweetened
Like aging wine
And where I lie, and nearby
New plants would surely grow
Their berries sweetened,
Their flowers brightened
By my overflow

If in years hence
You come to visit or to reside
And you see flowers blooming
Ripe, red berries
By their side,
You'll know I am still among the living
Not one of those
Who faded and died.

...T HER FATHER NEEDED ...
...U SEE SEE SHE HAD BEEN
...R QUITE A WHILE AND HE
...SAW HER SUFFERING AND
...E TOOK HER HOME TO G...
...I'S LOVING CARE TO STAY
...HERE, AND OH! HOW I M...
...NOW THAT SHE IS AWAY
...BEFORE SHE LEFT HE PROM...
...HAT IF W... ...EVE IN H...
...EE ALICE HER ...R DAY ...
...ATHERS HOUSE ARE MAN...
...ND HE IS PREPARING A...
...OR ME NOW, I'M GETTIN...
...O MOVE TO HIS HOUSE
...LIEE SOON I CA...
...PASS THROU...

Alice Doesn't Live Here Anymore

There is a knock at the door. I answer, and standing there is a little girl.

She asks, Is Alice home?

I answer,

No, I'm here alone. You see, Alice doesn't live here anymore. She has gone to live with her Father on that golden shore. She didn't want to leave us nor to grieve us, but her Father needed her more. You see she had been sick for quite a while and her Father saw her suffering and pain, so he took her home to give her his loving care, to stay with him there. And oh! How I miss her now that she is away. But before she left, he promised me that if we believe in him, I'll see her another day. For in our Father's house are many rooms and he is preparing a place for me now. I'm getting ready to move to his house to be with Alice soon. I can hardly wait to pass through those pearly gates and meet her there; that is my fervent prayer.

So little girl now you know where Alice and her Father are. It's not far, just beyond that star. Believe in him and he will let you in.

I fear that come ov

you will fade aw

And as the bubbl

Break and hide fr

my mirage

until t [QR code] fatal d

when [QR code] o aw

my heart will c

And as believers d

Have faith that

My mirage

My Mirage

In some of my poems, I can hear music or song. Probably corny to anyone else, but meaningful to me. This is one of them. I wish I could sing it for you.

I see your face
When you are near or far away
Most any place
Whether night or day
My mirage

Though others might not see
You are so real to me
No one could take your place
the touch of your embrace
My mirage

I fear that come one day
You will fade away
And as the bubbles do
Break and hide from view
My mirage

Until that fatal day
When you go away
My heart will cherish you
And as believers do
Have faith
Our love is true
My mirage

ALL DAY
WE CAN LAY HERE
PLAY AND PLAY

WHAT CAN WE DO
ON A DAY
LIKE THIS?

TENDERLY KISS & KISS
WHAT HEAVENLY BLISS
ON A DAY
LIKE THIS

WHAT CAN WE DO
ON A DAY
LIKE THIS?

SIT BY THE FIRE
WARMED BY OUR DESIRE
HOLDING HAND & TENDER
SHARING THE SWEETNESS
OUR LOVE PROFESSED

ON A DAY
LIKE THIS

To My Wife Alice on Nov 9, 1989

*You know how it can be on a dark dismal rainy
day in Southeast Alaska. The air is so wet and
damp you almost drown in breathing it in. There is
nothing on TV or radio; what do you do? There are
no neighbors or visitors, just you and the one you
love and who loves you. I wrote this for Alice. She
must have thought it somewhat important because
I found it in her personal drawer after she passed
away in January 2000.*

What can we do
On a day like this?
Storm clouds passing overhead
It's too cold to get out of bed

What can we do
On a day like this?
We can make love, all day
We can lay here, play and play

What can we do
On a day like this?
We can tenderly kiss and kiss
On a day like this

What can we do
On a day like this?
Sit by the fire
Warmed by our desire

Holding hands, with tender caresses
Sharing the sweetness
Our love professes
On a day like this

INKY PANKY, UNTIL I ...
NOTHER BASE IN WIESBADEN G...
POEM I GAVE HER WITH ...
ET-ME. NOTS 2D PICKED IN T...
- NAME WAS BOBBY MITC...
SEE THESE FLOWERS BOBBY
SPEAK THEM NOT!
BUT TO ME THEY SAY
YOUR AWFUL NICE
AND FORGET ME NOT
I FOUND ⬛⬛⬛ GROWIN...
DOWN B... LANE
AND AS =... THEM T...
THEY SEEMED TO SPEAK
YOUR NAME
SO HERE THEY ARE M...
I HOPE THEY BRING-YO...
AND WITH IT, THE ME...
FORGET ME NOT
FROM AN ADMIRING R...

Forget Me Not

In Berlin, I was working as a communications specialist (teletype operator) at Templehoff Airbase 1951-1952. I had noticed a Women's Air Force girl working in another section of the base. She looked interesting but I didn't know how to approach her. One day I noticed a small bunch of Forget-Me-Nots growing along the lawn going into the building. So I picked them and wrote this little poem, leaving it on her desk. After that we dated a little until I was transferred to another base in Wiesbaden, Germany.

See these flowers, Bobby?
Speak them not!
But to me they say
You're awful nice
And forget-me-not

I found them growing
Down by the lane
And as I saw them growing there
They seemed to speak your name

So here they are Miss Mitchell
I hope they bring you joy
And with it, the message
Forget me not
From this admiring boy

Friendship & Humor

BECOME PRESIDEN

D OTHERS

ERE It is & SISTE
        & BROTH

GUY

HE FIREWORK.

BANG

Tribute to Ivan Gamble, Sr.

The old home team won't be the same
with Ivan out of the game
Ivan was always ready to take the ball
and lead the team

Just when others were running out of steam
He'd carry the ball
Like at Christmas, he'd plan the program
and decorate the hall

And when sent, become President of Kootz-
noowoo,
A.N.B. and others
All Alaska people were his sisters and brothers

And on the Fourth of July, what a bang!
Ivan would buy the fireworks for the whole she-
bang

If there was ever a need
Ivan always took heed
and would lend a hand
Save the land!

For his native people, his creed
and his final deed

It will never be the same with Ivan out of the game

For he was our forward, our center, and our guard
The M.V.P., our star, the Captain of our team
and we are champs because of him.

6 December

Here in my southeast Alaska home
A thousand miles south of Nome
Sippin coffee from a steamin mug,
Warmed to the _bone_!
Outside I see.
Snows pilin up all around me
A beautiful sight to see,
But ice and Snows,
Are not for me!
The chill of frost filled air
Upon fingers, nose, or toes
for me
Does not _find_ fond feelings
Now that I am _old_,
I love being warm
Despise being cold.
Say,

Christmas 2003

It's December,
here in my Southeast Alaska home.
I'm snug as a bug in a rug,
a thousand miles or more south of Nome,
sippin' coffee from a steamin' mug;
warmed to the bone!

Outside I see snow pilin' up,
mountain tops glowin' white,
a beautiful sight to see,
But ice and snow are not for me!
The chill of frost filled air,
or bite upon my fingers, nose, or toes,
does not for me fond feelings invite!

Now that I am old,
I love being warm, despite being cold!
To all of you, I say to Hell with cold!
Bring me my slippers and old rockin' chair.
Place them close to the fire,
So that I can warm my fanny there,
Fill the room with family and friends,
tell tall tales throughout the long winter nights,
that seem to never end.
Better yet, give me a woman who glows!
Together, perhaps who knows, we can melt the ice and
snow.

Realistically speakin',
it is the sun I'll be seekin'
Come January one.
California, Arizona deserts I'll bike, walk and run,
Eating, drinkin', havin' fun,
Soaking up that warm southern sun.

This Christmas season,
my thoughts and wishes for you will be,
in this life and throughout all eternity,
Love, Health, and Prosperity
With knowledge of God's precious gift, Jesus his son.

...and wrinkles on m...
The sagging skins on my arm
The double chins,
A once straight and tall body
Now crookedly bent
The sharp memory, now,
Here, there, and went
Jet black and curly hair
What's left of it there
Now white as ... I touched snow
...know. Lik... it so long
...was young
...th day's tha... never seemed t...
...nance. Love and friends
...at me and see yourself
...you too will age
...a book. just turn a pag...

Frank W. It...

Turn The Page

Observe closely
The lines and wrinkles
In my face

The sagging skin on my arms
The double chins
A once straight and tall body
Now, crookedly bent

The sharp memory now
Here, there, and went
Jet black and curly hair
What's left of it there
Now white as untouched snow

And know, like you, not so long ago
I was young too. With days
That never seemed to end
Romance, love and friends

Look at me and
See yourself very soon
You too will age
Like a book, just turn the page.

we each live
in different little worlds
filled with problems
all our own

If each little world
would take the time
To understand his fellow man
wed be fine

when the road of life
Is full of woe
And their seems
No place to go

If each little world
would extend a hand
wed be

the creed of man
should always be
Love thy neihbor tenderly

If each little world
would obey the command
wed be fine

So starting here
with you and me

Little Worlds

We each live,
In different little worlds,
Filled with problems,
All our own

If each little world,
Would take the time,
To understand his fellow man,
We'd be fine

When the road of life,
Is full of woe,
And there seems,
No place to go

If each little world,
Would extend a hand,
We'd be fine

The creed of man,
Should always be,
Love thy neighbor tenderly

If each little world,
Would obey the command,
We'd be fine

So starting here,
With you and me,
Let's form a friendly
Family tree

One with arms,
All entwined,
And love one another,
All the time

. . . .
. . . .
. . . .
. . . .
. . . .
That grey Alaska Tux
And Fedora hat
With bent but sprightly gait
That no man
Can possibly keep up with
While biting steelhead wait.
Retiring Yes!
From the News releases
On how to oil your reel
And bait your line
Only so
He can giv. . . . .ell!
Fishing al. . . . . . . .ne.
Many a spil. . . . .
In the trec. . . . . . . .lave drove
Many a crab
Taken from a sheltered cove.
Many a hill hell climb
In quest of the wiley deer
Many a storm
The "Coaster" . . . .
Many a friend . . . .
any a tale . . . .
t. . .by
. . . . .
. . . . . .

Bob Bodie Retirement

He says he's retiring
But we all know
That's not so.
Just wait and see
Some stream --- somewhere
Fishing rod in hand,
He'll be there.
That grey Alaska tux
And fedora hat
That bent but sprightly gait
That no man
Can possibly keep up with
While biting steelhead wait.
Retiring yes!
From the news releases
On how to oil your reel
And bait your line
Only so
He can giv'er Hell!
Fishing all the time.
Many a spike
In the trees he'll have drove
Many a crab
Taken from a sheltered cove.
Many a hill he'll climb
In quest of the wiley deer
Many a storm
The "Coaster" through - He'll steer.
Many a friend he'll visit
Many a tale he'll tell
Of the day
The fishing was the best
Between you and me
If this is retiring
We all should make this our quest.

"Take Time"

...... of spring me...
...... since past,
... leaves of autumn
falling fast,
...... sounds of life-tim...
...ith quietly by
...owed on ... my friend...
that went ...... in,
as vain cookie ...ol...
in a war we ......
Time is running
Our frosting ......
take ......

Take Time

The greens of spring meadows
Are long since past
Golden leaves of Autumn
Are falling fast

The sands of lifetimes
Rush quickly by
Slowed only by friendships
That never die

As but vain cookie soldiers
Fighting a war we will never win
Time is running out
Our frosting is wearing thin

So take time, old friend
To sit and chat a spell
Of things past and future
Let us slow the tolling bell

We can slow the race
By having lunch today
So as to not injure old friendships past
You, of course, can pay!

~~of no~~ ~~bad~~ intentions.

~~Hidden~~ n within their lines.

The purpose of my prose,

Is to germinate friendship,

Just as the gardner plants h

~~to~~ planting seeds of friends

Among the fertil rows,

~~Watching as they bloom and~~

~~the~~ the ga [QR] 'aps what

A single flo [QR] a field,

~~without the~~ [QR] of anoth

~~empt~~ ~~will~~ not produce a yield.

~~So do~~ not take ^{not} my message

~~but does~~ not meet the

~~ake them as they are~~

~~Simple gesture.~~

~~and I hope~~ will festure

Messages Of Love

My messages of love
Relayed in rhyme
Have no underlying intentions
Hidden within their lines

The purpose of my prose
Is to germinate friendship
Among fertile rows
Watching as they bloom and multiply
For the gardener reaps what he sows

A single flower in a field
Without the pollen of another
Will not produce another yield

Do not take my messages of love
To imply
What does not meet the eye

Take them as they are
A simple gesture
I pray will foster
Love and understanding
Between human beings

Placed in Fertile Soil and given Tender care,
That once tiny Seed began to grow

Soon that tiny Seed sprouted Leaves,
Of Brilliant Greens, Blooms of many colors,
Ever Brightening my Life anew.

Filling to overflowing the empty Chambers,
Within my Lonely Heart.

What Joy that once tiny Seed brought to me,
Ever Ever filling my Soul with ecstasy

One Day I found that the precious Seed of Friendship
We planted together that other Day
Had withered and died
Forever gone from me

Oh! How I cried that fateful Day
When that Seed of Friendship slipped away

With tear filled eyes, I Cried as I had Cried
For other Loved ones who had passed my way
Emptying the fullness of the Pool
Of Compassion for Love contained within my Soul

A part of me Died that Day
When that tiny Seed of Friendship
Was forever taken from me

Seed of Friendship

A tiny seed of friendship
Was planted that glorious summer day.
Placed in fertile soil and given tender care,

That once tiny seed began to grow
Soon that tiny seed sprouted leaves,
Of brilliant greens, blooms of many colors,
Ever brightening my life anew.

Filling to overflowing the empty chambers,
Within my lonely heart,
What joy that once tiny seed brought to me,
Ever, ever filling my soul with ecstasy.

One day I found that the precious seed of friend-
ship
We planted on that summer day
Had wilted and died
Forever, ever taken from me

Oh! How I cried that fateful day,
When that seed of friendship slipped away.
With tear filled eyes. I cried as I had cried,
For other loved ones who had passed my way
Emptying the fullness of the pool
Of compassion for love contained within my soul.

a as a ...

flow without restriction bend

Push it to its limit

And youll find it never

savor it as you w

good food

value i o-th fo

than pri gems

Its not a temporary

or just a sudden

It isnt given to

passerby

Friendship

Trust in my friendship!

Consider it as a road
That never ends
As a river whose waters flow
Without bends

Push it to the limits
Savor it as you would
Good food
You will find
It is not a temporary thing
Or just a sudden mood

Treat it as you would
a precious stone
For it is seldom given
And is yours alone

time will [...]
sure as you are yo[u]
I am I

[n]ow I wish I'd list[...]
done as I was to
Now mothers your
I am growing ol[d]

my chil[d] I am s[...]
kind [...] and s[...]
[re]member shes your
[an]d he is your br[...]
[an]d time will sw[...]
sure as you are
[an]d I am I.

FC

She Used to Say (1976)

Mother went to heaven
Four years ago today
But I can still remember
The things she used to say

Remember she's your sister
And he is your brother
Be kind to one another
For time will swiftly fly
As sure as you are you
And I am I

Oh how I wish I'd listened
And done as I was told
For now mother's gone
And I am growing old

To my children I am saying
Be kind to one another
Remember she's your sister
And he is your brother
And time will swiftly fly
As sure as you are you
And I am I

where the sun always sh[ines]
in that promised land
without the cares and wha[t]
the rain and snows and e[verything]
else that goes. with the co[ld]
boats
well old friend though you[ve]
stated no boats for me
I'm afraid your fated
she's a t█████tle shi[p]
that reg████ittle ca[re]
and if y█████k close
you~~ll find~~ that martin[y]
so. safe journey and go[od]
sailing old sport
your berth always a[waits]
you at this port.

Frank

Ed Bowman Retirement (1968)

You thought you'd get away
To that great southland
Where the sun always shines
In that promised land

Without the cares and woes
The rain and snows
and everything else that goes
with the care of boats

Well old friend
Though you've always stated
"No boats for me"
I'm afraid you're fated

She's a trim little ship
That requires little care
And if you'll look close enough
You'll find that martini there

So safe journey and
Good sailing old sport
Your berth always awaits
You at this port.

Berlin

...ow you see it ?
...hope you can
see it spinning fast
...ybe faster than a fan?
e your hair is curly
it grow all alone?
cuse me for
t you hea   minute
five   phone
about   vow
a loan ?
ear Honey near
the Bar ?
leave ?

ll be going now
lost ready

Can You See It?

Can you see it?
I hope you can
See it spinning fast,
Maybe faster than a fan?

Gee your hair is curly,
Did it grow all alone?
Excuse me for a minute please,
Can't you hear the phone?

I'm fine you know,
How about a loon?
I hear honey near,
At the bar?
Casaleone?

Guess I'll be going now,
They're almost ready
Ho! jump, whoops, steady!

STRAIGHT AND TALL
AS THOUGH.
HE DIDN'T KNOW
HE WASN'T SUPPOSED
TO STAND AT ALL
AND WHILE
ALL OF THE OTHER
WALKE[...] QUICKLY
TO A [...]RO
THIS ONE LEGGE[...]
HOPPED
TO WHERE HE WA[...]
"STAS THOUGH
HE DIDN'T KNOW
HE WAS A ONE LE[...]

One Legged Crow

Today
I saw a one legged crow
Standing on one leg
Straight and tall
As though he did not know
He wasn't supposed to stand at all

While all the other crows
Walked briskly to and fro
This one legged crow
Hopped on one leg
To where he wanted to go!

Just as though
He did not know
He was a one legged crow

just an acto...
the play of life.
part I play is not...
I go through each l...
established by the scrip...
peaking and moving as...
the part I play,
it its not from my...
I see myself upon thi...
portraying ... the image of...
Going thr... the mot...
As Directe... the li...
And at ... trodding o...
But its not me I se...
I should win the Ac...
For this part I play...
Each Line Done with...
The character,
Giving an admirable...
which leaves the au...

Play of Life

I am just an actor
In the play of life
For the part I play
Is not me

Oh! I go through each line
Moving and speaking
As required by the script

Each line done with perfection
Leaving my audience
With the impression
That the part I play
Is really me

Unlike an actor
Upon the stage or screen
I cannot change to another role
For the part of life is the part
I must play

This role of life I am cast in
Continues without acclaim or reviews
Until the final curtain call
The audience unaware
The perfect part I have played.

Ive got a story to tell!
Ive got a story to tell!
If you don't want to listen
You can go to --- well ---
I went down to this little tow...
Just to give them a run-aro...
All I wanted was a bottle of
But the man said, How'd you her...
The Federal Government has made it
To drink anything other than ora...
I'm going to [QR] turn you
And ask yo[QR] ave this h...
Well, I did. [QR] what to d...
As I turned away I heard
him say
          Orang/lime. It's real
       Drink it warm. Drink it
          Any old time. It's re
          I Drink it myself all t

~~I drink~~
f you should ever have t...

Orange/Lime

I've got a story to tell!
I've got a story to tell!
If you don't want to listen
You can go to... well...

I went down to this little town
Just to give them a run around
All I wanted was a bottle of booze
But the man said, haven't you heard the news?

The Federal Government has made it a crime
To drink anything other than Orange/Lime
I'm going to have to turn you down
And ask you to leave this here town...

Well I didn't know what to do,
I didn't know what to say
And as I turned away
I heard the little man say

Orange/Lime, it's real nice
Drink it warm, drink it with ice
Any old time, it's real fine
I drink it myself all the time!

Well if you should ever have to go
To a little town in Idaho
Remember how I told you so
And remember this little rhyme

Orange/Lime, it's real nice
Drink it warm, drink it with ice
Any old time, it's real fine
I drink it myself all the time!

Wilderness & Spirit

night's me rainbow.
Dancing in the cold
northern sky.
Pirouetting,
Holding Hands,
music played
by silent Bands,
upon a stage
That fills the eye----
The northern sky

Ever changing Hues
Reds, Yellows, blues,
Respond, upon
a Direct --
Sometim
Sometim
Flashing!
Across the sky
In the northern Night

Ever changing patterns
never repeated twice
some say
Reflections of in lig
upon the northern ic

Aurora Borealis (1977)

Nighttime rainbows
Dancing in the cold Northern skies
Pirouetting, holding hands
Music played by silent bands
Upon a stage that fills the eye
The Northern sky

Ever changing hues
Reds, greens, yellows, blues
Responding as upon
A director's cues
Sometimes dim
Sometimes bright
Flashing across the sky
In the Northern night

Ever changing patterns
Never repeated twice
Some say reflections of sun rays
Upon the Arctic ice.

Oh man!
With all your worldly feats
None can match
This treat of treats
That fills one with pure delight
The show of shows
The Aurora Borealis
Northern Lights.

of snow capped mou[...]
The lake lies calm
and black
except for an occasio[...]
from unknown sources
The crescent moon
Has been rising abo[...]
Golden yellow
Though it is not y[...]
The air [...]-old
and al[...] be cl[...]
A time to reflect
on things
past and futur[...]
what peace I f[...]
At a time
And place
[...]th[...]

All is Quiet

All is quiet
Except for the roar
Of a distant stream

Tall mountains tower above me
Shaded from dark greens
At the lake water's edge
To the bright whites
Of snow covered mountain tops

The lake lies calm and black
Except for an occasional ripple
From unknown sources

A crescent moon
Has been rising above me
Golden yellow
Though it is not yet night
The air is cold
And all can be plainly seen

A time to reflect
On things past and future
What peace! I find
At a time and place
Such as this

The life you gave ...
Each Tree, every exsisting thing,
Including me

I hear the Birds singing,
Their Songs of Praise,
See the Sun and Moon,
Rising and Setting,
Separating Nights from Days.

I smell the Forests fragrances,
Hear the Winds,
Whistling, through the Trees,
Your wonders all,
Bringing me often to my Knees.

I am exillera... ...ed exactly,
Upon your G... ...u,
As they shou...
The Master Gardner,
Perfect! just as you are perfect.

Thank you Lord! Thank you!,
For allowing me,
To live my Early Life,
Where their are still places,
Only your Eyes have seen,
Only your Hands have touched.

Thank you Lord! Thank you!,
By your Grace, for allowing me,
To dwell, in this special place.

In This Special Place

I feel your presence in my soul
I see your wonders with my eyes
The life you gave each plant
Each tree, every existing thing
Including me

I hear the birds singing
Their songs of praise
See the sun and moon
Rising and setting
Separating nights from days

I smell the forest's fragrance
Hear the winds
Whistling through the trees
Your wonders all
Bringing me often to my knees

I am exhilarated as I gaze
Upon your gardens, placed exactly
As they should be, by you
The Master Gardener
Perfect! Just as you are perfect.

Thank you, Lord! Thank you!
By your grace
For allowing me to dwell
In this special place

The souls of our lo[...]
Have been carrie[...]
We know you are a[...]
In our times of [...]
With your Great, G[...]
Although we do not [...]
For, we are but m[...]
We have faith in y[...]
of J[...]eat Crea[...]
To th[...]at are h[...]
Heal thier aching h[...]
Mend thier broker[...]
Fill them Lord, wit[...]
Give them your w[...]
Let them hear it[...]
Your Great C[...]

Remember

Let us always remember that day,
The eleventh of September,
When on the wings of three great white planes,
Come suffering and pain to all nations,
From the skies above.
Although the buildings now lie in rubble,
The souls of our loved ones, this day,
Have been carried away.
We know you are always with us,
In our times of trouble,
With your great, great love from above.
Although we do not understand your master plan,
For, we are but man,
We have faith in your word and have heard
Of your great, great love from above.
To those that are hurting, Lord,
Heal their aching hearts,
Mind their broken parts,
Fill them Lord, with your Holy Spirit,
Give them your word Lord,
Let them hear it!
Your great, great love, from above.

Christmas 1998

It is the season!

Everywhere
Merry Christmas
And favorite carols
Fill the air

Gaily decorated
Yards and houses
Draped with multi-colored lights

Santa on rooftops
and Christmas trees
Much to everyone's delight

Children, and adults too!
Their eyes all aglow
Dream of presents
And gently falling snow

While parents shop for gifts
In the shopping marts
Busily filling Santa's stockings
In their overloaded shopping carts

It is a festive season
As it should be
But not because of Santa
Or for the Christmas tree

For it is His birth
Ne'r forget
On this date
We celebrate

So shout it from the rooftops!
Sing songs of praise!
For all who accept Him King
From the dead, he shall raise

A gift so precious
Given absolutely free
A zillion times more meaningful
Than hoards of presents
Under the Christmas tree

Put Christ back into Christmas
Glorify not Rudolf or Santa Claus
In your merriment this joyous season
Take time out to pause...

To some, it may seem outlandish
But the truth is, in Spanish, it seems
Christmas actually means
More Christ!

Put Christ back into Christmas.

HAVE YOU EVER SEEN
THE PHOSPHORESANCE
OF THE SEA
ON A DARK WINTERS NIGHT!?
WHEN STIRRED SO VIOLENTLY
IT PRODUC[...]LEAMING
WHITE LI[...]
AND ALL [...]
AS BRIGHT AS DAY?
ITS AWE INSPIRING
IS ALL I CAN SAY!

Phosphorescence

Have you ever seen
The phosphorescence
Of the sea
On a dark winter's night
When stirred so violently
It produces a gleaming
White light
And all is lit
As bright as day?!

It's awe inspiring
Is all I can say!

WE ARE TLINGIT. THE ORIGINAL PEO
OF ADMIRALTY ISLAND

OUR ISLANDS FERTILE SOILS AND WATER
HAVE ALWAY'S FED US WHEN WE WERE
HUNGRY, QUELLED OUR THIRSTS WHEN
THIRSTY,

GIVEN US COMFORT IN IT'S VERY WILDNE
IN THE SOLITUDE OF NATURES s̶t̶i̶l̶l̶
SINCE THE BEGINING OF t̶h̶e̶s̶e̶. CREATI

THE SPIRITS OF OUR FOREFATHERS SPEAK
TO US STILL, JUST AS THIER SPIRITS T
TO THE MOTHE ___ OICES ECHOING
LOUDLY THRO ___ WINDSWEPT
A
T̶H̶E̶ OCEANS S ___ HING ON t̶h̶e̶ THE
ROCKY ISLA ___ E. IN THE SO
GENTLY FALLING RAIN.

SAYING TO US!
"YOU ARE MY PEOPLE!
I GIVE YOU THESE LANDS AND ALL TH
THINGS BENEATH THESE LANDS IN
WATERS; FRESH & SALT, I GIVE YOU
THE THINGS THAT WALK ON THESE LAND
THE SKY'S ABOVE THESE LANDS. THE M___E
H LIE BELOW THESE LANDS FOR YOU
b̶▢̶PROSPER. FOR YOU TO PROSPE

We Are Tlingit

We are Tlingit, the original people of Admiralty Island. Our island's fertile soils and waters have always fed us when we were hungry, quelled our thirsts when we were thirsty. Given us comfort in it's very wildness, in the solitude of nature since the beginning of creation.

The spirits of our forefathers speak to us still, just as their spirits talked to them. The spirits voice echoing loudly throughout a windswept forest, the ocean surf crashing on the rocky island shore, in the sound of gently falling rain.

Saying to us! You are my people!

I give you these lands and all the things beneath these lands and beneath the waters. I give you all the things that walk on these lands and fly on the skies above. The minerals that lie below these lands for you to use and for you to prosper.

I give you these things to feed you. To keep you warm and dry. To keep you safe. To keep you from being sad, hungry, or thirsty.

I say to you RESPECT these things I give you.

I say to you PROTECT these things I give to you.

PROTECT them as you would protect a friend, your family, your children!

I give you these things as I gave you your mother, to nurse you when you were hungry, to comfort you when you were lonely or sad.

Let no earthly thing take from you what I have given in love, for you, my people!

I Got Lost

I got lost! And I've been up to that place. It's not far. You just go up and boom, you're down in this meadow, this lake, you own the whole thing. But there was 40 inches of snow! My son dropped me off, I'm going up the hill, I've been there lots of times. I've trapped beaver there, I've shot deer there, the whole thing. And the first thing I know, you can't see anything! Everything is different! There's no hills to look at, there's nothing there. It's just a straight line. I'd given my compass, which I wouldn't have used anyway, to my granddaughter.

The first thing I know, I get back in there and I can't find the thing. Usually you just go up and then you go down into the thing, there it is! For 3 days and 2 nights I wandered. At night I stayed by the meadow, because I had a good flashlight, thinking I could signal. I knew I could find the drainage… if you find a drainage you can follow it down. I'd go and I'd find a lake or something, but you're talking about snow, heavy snow, it was even snowing then. I'd go to one end of the lake and there wouldn't be any drainage! And it wouldn't be an easy walk over the lake. I'd get to the other side, no drainage! And so I just wandered, I wandered, going around. Nothing visual to give me any location, like the hill behind or anything. So I just walked and walked and walked and walked. On the last night, I was standing at this meadow I would go by with my really good flashlight, thinking that if a helicopter were to come I could signal it. I was standing there, and I'm going to tell you - I saw people. I was standing there, I would stand up all night, and I would fall asleep and fall over like a log. WHAM! I'd hit the ground. I couldn't start a fire or anything with no wood. I'm standing there, and from about the distance of here to my shed down there, I'd see this girl, standing at the edge of the meadow. She's got on a white hat, she's blonde, and she's got on a black dress with a white design and red boots. So I thought, "What the heck is that?" And I know I'm not hallucinating… I'm good! I'd do arm flaps and jumping jacks and things like that, that's how I kept warm. And so I'm really curious, what the heck? And I'd start walking out towards her, and then I'd shine the light. And she was standing there, with her arms outstretched and her fingers moving. When I would come a bit closer, she'd turn, smile at me, and turn back to doing what she was doing again. She'd turn, look at me, smile, and then go back.

In the background, a little further, maybe to the trees, there was a couple, a man and a girl. They didn't pay attention to me, really. They'd go around, like they were dancing. But that girl, every time I'd go out, she'd have her arms out, her fingers moving, and she'd turn and smile at me. I went out several times. One time I was standing there, and I heard the 9pm Alaska Airlines flight. I see it every night, Seattle to Anchorage. AHA! I know where west is. That's west, so I've got to go this way. So the next morning, I headed west, found a drainage, a tough one, wide, snow on top, water under, logs over it… I was going down the drainage, knew where I was, and I heard voices. I ran into the search team coming up. 20 minutes more I would have been on the beach. I think that girl was pointing the way out. What she was doing, where she was pointing, that was the way out. Honest.

There where 60 people out looking for me, including my son. And I just walked out, went down to the team, they put me in a boat, brought me over to the airplane float. They had an ambulance and a stretcher there, they say they want to take me up and check me out at the clinic. I say, "I'm not getting in that stretcher, and I'm not getting in that ambulance. I'm walking home." That's the way I am. I was in good shape! I did get frostbite in my toes, that was all the damage I had.